D0786219

8941

Johnson, Sylvia A.

Mosses

DATE DUE

hool
ct

MOSSES

MOSSES

by Sylvia A. Johnson

Photographs by Masana Izawa

A Lerner Natural Science Book

Lerner Publications Company ▪ Minneapolis

Sylvia A. Johnson, Series Editor

Translation of original text by Yasuhiko Katagiri

The publisher wishes to thank Pietra Gardetto,
Botany Department, University of Minnesota,
for her assistance in the preparation of this book.

Photograph on page 9 (upper right) by Susumu Kanozawa

The glossary on pages 45 and 46 gives definitions and pronunciations of words shown in **bold type** in the text. An explanation of the scientific names used in this book appears on page 47.

LIBRARY OF CONGRESS CATALOGING IN PUBLICATION DATA

Johnson, Sylvia A.
 Mosses.

  (A Lerner natural science book)
  Adaptation of: Koke no sekai / Masana Izawa.
  Includes index.
  Summary: Describes the characteristics and development of mosses.
  1. Mosses—Juvenile literature. [1. Mosses] I. Izawa, Masana, ill. II. Izawa, Masana. Koke no sekai. III. Title. IV. Series.
 QK537.5.J63 1983   588'.2   83-17488
 ISBN 0-8225-1482-6 (lib. bdg.)

International Standard Book Number: 0-8225-1482-6
Library of Congress Catalog Card Number: 83-17488

  2 3 4 5 6 7 8 9 10 91 90 89 88 87 86 85 84

When you are hiking in the woods or along the bank of a quiet stream, you may find yourself walking on a thick green mat of living plants. This natural carpet clings close to the earth and feels soft and springy under your feet. If you get down on your knees and look at the carpet closely, you will see that it is made up of thousands of individual shoots, each with its own stem and leaves. These tiny living things are mosses, very special members of the plant kingdom.

Mosses grow in many kinds of places. They can be found on the trunks and branches of living trees or on dead stumps and logs. Many mosses grow on moist ground, in meadows or near freshwater ponds and streams. Moss can even grow on rock and cement.

7

The kingdom of plants is very large and very complex. It includes more than 350,000 kinds of living plants, ranging from tiny one-celled algae to sunflowers and giant cypress trees. Mosses are more complicated in their structure than algae, but they are much simpler than trees and flowering plants like sunflowers. By comparing mosses to representatives of some other plant groups, we can get a better idea of what they are like.

Like sunflowers, trees, ferns, and many other kinds of green plants, mosses are able to produce their own food through the process of **photosynthesis.** This sets them apart from another group of simple plants, the fungi. Fungi like mushrooms do not contain **chlorophyll,** the essential ingredient for food production. They must obtain nourishment from other plants.

Mosses are different from fungi in the way they obtain food, but the two groups do have some similarities. The most important is their method of reproduction. Neither mosses nor mushrooms grow from seeds, as many other kinds of familiar plants do. Instead they reproduce by means of **spores,** tiny one-celled structures that are much simpler than seeds. Liverworts are close relatives of mosses that also produce spores instead of seeds. Ferns are more distantly related but have a similar method of reproduction.

In the next few pages, we will take a look at the fascinating and complicated system by which mosses produce more of their own kind.

Mosses (upper left), mushrooms (below), and ferns (below) are all seedless plants that reproduce by means of spores. Sunflowers (upper right) and other flowering plants grow from seeds. Flowering plants, like mosses and ferns, produce food through photosynthesis, while mushrooms and other fungi are unable to make their own food.

These two moss plants are in the gametophyte stage of their reproductive cycle.

Mosses go through two very different stages in their reproductive cycles. During these two stages, moss plants have different forms and they function in different ways. The scientific name for this two-stage system of reproduction is **alternation of generations.**

The leafy little moss plants that we usually see growing on trees or on the ground represent the sexual generation or stage of moss development. At the tips of the leafy shoots are located reproductive organs that produce male and female sex cells. Sex cells are also known as **gametes,** and the moss plant in this stage is called a **gametophyte,** or gamete-producing plant.

In some kinds of mosses, the male reproductive organ, called an **antheridium,** grows on one plant, while the female organ, or **archegonium,** grows on another. Other kinds of mosses have both sex organs on the same plant.

10

Right: Male reproductive organs develop inside the cups at the tips of these moss shoots. *Below:* Female organs form at the tips of these slender shoots.

Left: **Antheridia of the green felt moss** *(Pogonatum inflexum). Above:* **Sperm are produced inside the cup formed by the petal-like leaves.**

The male organs of many kinds of mosses are surrounded by special leaves that resemble flower petals. Inside the little cup formed by these leaves develop large numbers of male sperm cells. Each female reproductive organ has a hollow base in which a single egg cell develops.

In order for sexual reproduction to take place, the egg cell produced by the female organ must be united with a male sperm cell. In flowering plants, this union is often brought about by insects that carry pollen containing male sperm cells to the female organ of the flower. In mosses, the sperm cells are carried by water.

12

Above: A fertilized egg cell inside a female archegonium. This cell is the first stage in the development that will produce the sporophyte generation of the moss plant (right).

Moss sperm cells are equipped with whip-like tails that enable them to swim. When a moss plant is wet with dew or rain, the sperm burst from the antheridia and swim through the thin film of water toward the archegonia. They are attracted by a chemical produced by the female organs.

A single sperm cell enters each archegonium and unites with the egg cell it contains. This union is known as **fertilization,** and it is the beginning of the next stage of the moss reproductive cycle. After fertilization, the moss plant is no longer a producer of gametes, or sex cells. It is now a **sporophyte**—a producer of spores.

Inside the female archegonium, the fertilized egg cell starts its development. As the cell divides to form more and more cells, the young sporophyte moss begins to take shape.

The sporophyte grows directly out of the leafy female gametophyte. As it becomes larger, it forms a leafless stalk, or **seta,** that connects it to the female plant. At the tip of the seta, a kind of capsule or case develops. This is the part of the sporophyte that will produce spores.

The pictures on these two pages show the sporophytes of several different mosses. They have been greatly enlarged so that you can see the slender stalks with the spore capsules at their tips.

14

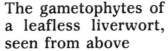

The gametophytes of a leafless liverwort, seen from above

The green plants known as liverworts are close relatives of mosses and reproduce in much the same way. They also have a gametophyte stage that leads to the development of sporophytes. Some liverworts have leafy gametophytes that look a lot like mosses, but others lack leaves and stems. The gametophytes of leafless liverworts grow flat against the ground and look something like little pieces of green ribbon.

One of the most common of these leafless liverworts is a small plant known by the scientific name *Marchantia* (mar-SHAN-tee-uh). When a *Marchantia* liverwort is ready to reproduce, male and female sex organs develop on separate stalks that extend above the main part of the plant. At the top of the stalks are little umbrella-shaped structures (shown on the opposite page). Female archegonia develop

16

Left: The female "umbrellas" of *Marchantia* grow on long stalks above the main part of the plant. *Right:* The scalloped male "umbrellas" grow on shorter stalks.

on the underside of the female "umbrellas," which are divided into finger-like sections, or lobes. Male antheridia form on top of the scalloped male "umbrellas."

Fertilization in *Marchantia* and other liverworts takes place in the same way as in mosses, with the tiny sperm swimming through a film of water to unite with the female eggs. The fertilized eggs then develop into liverwort sporophytes. In *Marchantia,* the sporophytes grow on the underside of the female umbrella. They look very different from the tall, slender moss sporophytes, but they have the same parts and function in the same way.

Let's take a look at these two kinds of plants in the sporophyte stage of their reproductive cycles.

Leaves

CALYPTRA

SETA

SPORO-
PHYTE

FOOT

GAMETO-
PHYTE

Capsules

Stems

Rhizoids

This is a green felt moss *(Pogonatum inflexum)* of the spore-producing generation. The long, slender seta of the sporophyte rises out of the female gametophyte. At its tip is the spore capsule. As you can see in the photograph, the capsule has a little pointed cap on top. This cap, called the **calyptra,** is the upper part of the female archegonium in which the sporophyte began its development. It will fall off when the spores in the capsule are ready to be released.

The sporophyte is connected to the stem of the parent gametophyte by a structure called the **foot,** located at the base of the seta. It is through this structure that the sporophyte absorbs food from the parent plant.

The thin stem of the moss gametophyte is connected to a mass of root-like threads, or **rhizoids.** Unlike the roots of more complicated plants, rhizoids serve mainly to anchor the moss to the earth rather than to take in moisture and nourishment.

The leafless gametophyte of a *Marchantia* liverwort (below) is also anchored to the earth by rhizoids. Out of the gametophyte rises the thin stalk that bears the female umbrella, with its graceful lobes. The tiny liverwort sporophytes, developing from the fertilized eggs, hang from the underside of the umbrella like little bags. Just like a moss sporophyte, each is made up of a capsule, a seta, and a foot that connects it to the parent gametophyte.

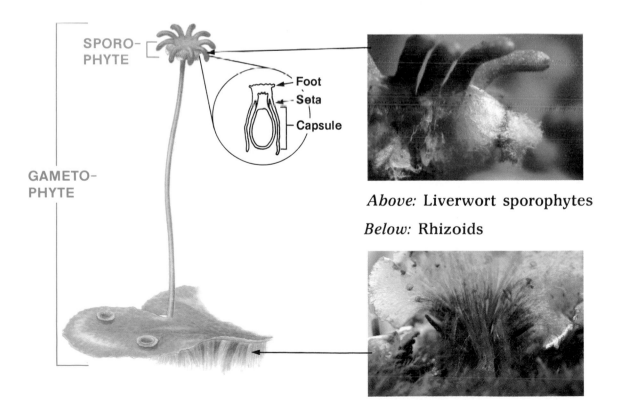

SPORO-
PHYTE

Foot
Seta
Capsule

GAMETO-
PHYTE

Above: Liverwort sporophytes

Below: Rhizoids

Swaying on their slender stalks, moss spore capsules stand high above the leafy shoots of the parent gametophytes.

As a sporophyte develops, thousands of tiny spores form within its capsule. When the spores become ripe, they are ready to be released. Different kinds of mosses and liverworts have complicated methods of releasing their spores.

In order for moss spores to escape, the opening in the top of the sporophyte capsule must be uncovered. In most mosses, this opening is covered not only by the calyptra but also by a tight-fitting lid called the **operculum,** which is under the calyptra.

Both the calyptra and the operculum usually fall off before the spores are ready to be released. But the opening of the capsule is still not free of coverings. Underneath the operculum is a structure made up of many tiny pointed teeth. This structure is known as the **peristome,** from two Greek words meaning "around the mouth."

The teeth of the peristome form a ring around the mouth or opening of the spore capsule. When the teeth are locked together, as in the photograph on the left, they seal the opening and prevent spores from getting out. When the teeth of the peristome separate, as shown on the opposite page, the opening of the spore case is unsealed and the spores are able to escape.

Above: The teeth of these moss peristomes are long and thin. When the peristome is closed, the teeth come together to form a point (left). When the teeth separate, the opening of the spore capsule is uncovered (right).

Right: The closed peristome of the cord moss *(Funaria hygrometrica)* looks something like the shutter of a camera. Scientists often identify different kinds of mosses by the structure of their peristomes and the number of teeth they contain.

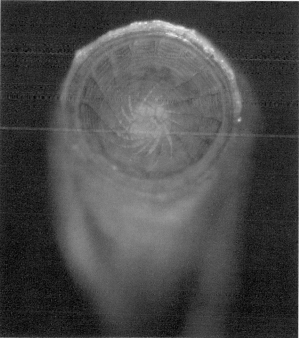

The green-colored spores (below) of the green felt moss are released by the wind (left).

The movement of the peristome is usually controlled by moisture. Under humid conditions, the teeth of the peristome expand and lock together, sealing the spore capsule. This prevents moisture from getting into the capsule. It also keeps the spores from being released in damp weather, when they would become heavy with moisture and fall to the ground instead of being scattered by the wind.

Dry weather provides ideal conditions for spore dispersal. During dry periods, the teeth of the peristome tighten, uncovering the opening of the capsule. The slightest breeze will sway the flexible seta and tip the spores out the opening. In some mosses, the teeth of the peristome actually help to disperse the spores. In humid weather, the tips of the teeth dip down into the capsule. When it is dry, the teeth straighten up, lifting spores out and flinging them away.

24

The spore capsules of a *Marchantia* liverwort (above) contain twisted threads (right) that help to disperse the spores.

Liverworts like *Marchantia* have a different method of scattering their spores. Their spore capsules contain twisted threads that act like springs. In dry conditions, the capsules split open and the threads uncoil, shooting the spores out.

Once the dust-like spores are out of the capsules, they are carried away by the wind to begin the next stage in the plant's development.

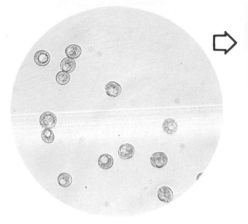

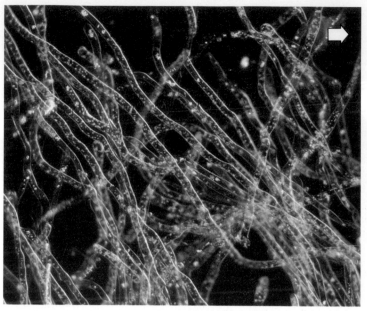

Microscopic moss spores (above) develop into the thread-like protonema (right).

The next stage of development is a new generation of gametophytes, which will grow from the spores produced by the sporophyte. If a spore lands in a place with sufficient moisture and warmth, it will germinate, or begin to grow. The single cell that makes up the spore divides to form many new cells. Eventually the spore develops into a thread-like structure known as the **protonema.**

The protonema branches out in many directions, spreading over the ground. Soon small **buds** begin to appear on the branches. These buds will develop into the leafy shoots of the gametophyte generation. When the shoots become mature, male and female reproductive organs will develop on their tips and the whole cycle of reproduction will begin again.

As the protonema grows and spreads over the ground (right), small buds begin to appear (above). The buds eventually develop into the leafy shoots of the gametophyte generation (below).

THE REPRODUCTIVE CYCLE OF A MOSS

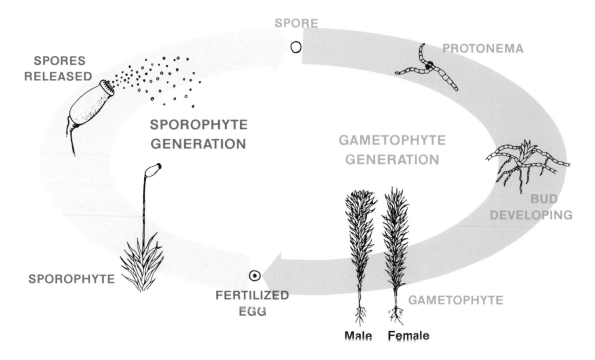

The two-stage cycle that produces new mosses and liverworts is complicated, and there are many things that can go wrong. If there are not enough male and female gametophytes growing in the same area, the chances of fertilization taking place are slim. Lack of moisture can also prevent the male sperm cells from reaching the female egg cells.

To avoid these and other problems, many mosses and liverworts have developed the ability to reproduce asexually (without the union of sex cells). These plants can make more of their own kind through the process of **vegetative propagation,** in which a new gametophyte grows directly from part of an existing gametophyte.

The gemmae of *Marchantia* liverworts develop in little cups.

In vegetative propagation, the new gametophytes usually develop from specialized pieces of plant tissue known as **gemmae.** Moss gemmae form at the tips of the leafy gametophyte shoots. The gemmae of *Marchantia* develop in little cups that grow on the flat body of the liverwort plant. They look something like tiny eggs enclosed in nests (shown in the picture above).

If a gemma breaks off and falls on moist ground, its cells begin to divide and to produce protonema. Buds forming on the protonema will then develop into another generation of gametophytes.

Right and below: Moss gemmae growing at the tips of gametophyte shoots. They are connected to the gametophytes by short stalks that break easily.

Whether it develops from a gemma or a spore, a moss plant must grow in the right kind of environment or it will not be able to continue its development. The most important element in a moss's environment is moisture.

All plants must have moisture in order to survive. Water is one of the essential ingredients in the process of photosynthesis, through which green plants make food. A seed plant draws water from the soil through its roots. The precious moisture is carried to all parts of the plant by a complicated **vascular system** made up of tiny tubes. But mosses do not have true roots or well-developed vascular systems. Their water supply depends on the moisture that falls on the surface of their leaves and stems.

Many mosses get the moisture they need by growing in a continuously damp environment—in or near a body of water or in an area of heavy rainfall. Thus mosses are common in marshy regions or in humid forests and woodlands.

In woodland areas where moisture is particularly high, you can find a wonderland of mosses. One such area is located on the Pacific coast of North America in northern Washington and southern British Columbia. Here heavy rainfall has created a temperate rain forest where trees and other green plants grow luxuriantly. Mosses drape the branches of trees and hang down in thick curtains. Fallen logs are covered by soft green blankets of living plants.

This rock-growing moss gets the moisture it needs from the splashing waters of a stream.

Since mosses do not need to draw moisture from the soil, they can grow on many kinds of surfaces. Mosses attach themselves not only to tree bark but also to rock, gravel, concrete, or brick. Thus you may find patches of moss growing on rocks in your backyard or on a damp wall in your basement.

A moss's thread-like rhizoids cling to such hard surfaces, establishing a foothold for the plant. As the moss grows, it builds up a tangled network of stems and leaves that collect moisture and nutrients from the air. With these resources, hardy rock-growing mosses can live very successfully in places where other plants could not survive.

Because mosses can survive in such harsh environments, they plan an important role in preparing the way for other plants with more complicated growing requirements. Over the years, mosses growing on rocks can actually crumble the hard substance, creating new soil. The tangled mats of mosses also collect particles of soil and other materials that form a bed suitable for the growth of ferns and other root plants.

Many mosses play an important role as "pioneer" plants— the first living things that appear in areas where the natural environment has been disturbed or damaged in some way. For example, cord moss as well as the *Marchantia* liverwort grow well in areas that have been burned over. You will frequently find these plants around the sites of old campfires.

Two kinds of moss clinging to a rocky hillside

Purple horn-toothed moss *(Ceratodon purpureus)* forms an attractive covering for an old straw roof.

The purple horned-tooth moss (shown in the picture above) is often a pioneer in disturbed soil like that formed when highways are built. If you look at the gravelly banks along a new superhighway, you might see mile-long stretches of this purple-colored moss. The clumps of moss help to hold the loose soil in place. At the same time, they begin the healing process that will eventually turn the disturbed area into a healthy environment for other plants.

Some mosses are even tough enough to survive in environments low in moisture. These mosses can live through droughts or grow in desert areas because they have a remarkable ability to go without water for long periods of time.

36

The tough little fork moss *(Dicranella heteromalla)* can even be found growing in crevices near the lava flow from a volcano.

When they are deprived of water, these hardy mosses become very dry. Their leaves curl up and turn brown or black. The mosses seem to be dead, but they are quickly revived by a rainfall. When they receive a new supply of water, their color returns and they continue producing food and growing. Scientists have tested these amazing mosses in the laboratory and have found that some of them can survive for as long as 9 or 10 years without water.

Of all the kinds of mosses, the sphagnums (SFAG-nuhms) are probably the ones that have played the biggest role in human life. Over the centuries, people have put these plants to many different uses.

One characteristic that makes sphagnum so useful is its ability to absorb moisture. The leaves of the moss contain not only food-manufacturing cells but also hollow cells that take in water from the surface of the plant. A sphagnum moss can absorb up to 20 percent of its own weight in water.

Because it can retain so much moisture, sphagnum is often used by gardeners as a packing material for fragile plants. Spread on a garden, the moss helps to keep moisture in the soil. During World War I, dried sphagnum was used for a very different purpose—as an absorbent dressing for wounds.

Even more important than these practical uses, sphagnum plays a significant role in changing the natural environment. Sphagnum mosses usually grow in very wet areas, on the edges of shallow lakes and ponds. As they develop, the mosses form thick mats that extend out over the surface of the water. At the top of the mats are the green living plants, while underneath are layers of dead leaves and stems tangled with soil and material from other plants.

Over the years, a sphagnum mat can expand until it extends from shore to shore, turning the lake into a **bog**. Shrubs and even trees take root and grow on the thick, spongy mat. If a human or animal walks on it, the floating sphagnum mat will tremble but it will hold firm. Eventually the sphagnum may fill the whole basin of the lake with vegetation.

Above: The leaves of sphagnum mosses vary in color from light green to pink and reddish brown. *Below:* Sphagnum growing in thick mats around a quiet pond

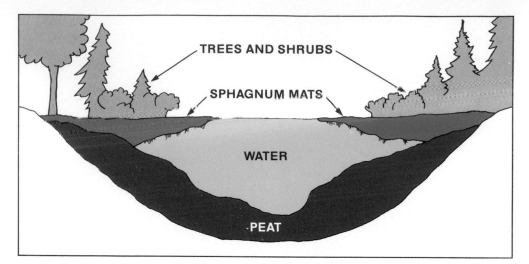

Above: This drawing shows how the growth of sphagnum mosses creates a bog. *Opposite:* The deep green of a sphagnum moss *(Sphagnum macrophyllum)* contrasts with the color of autumn leaves floating on a woodland stream.

The layer of dead plants at the bottom of the mass of sphagnum becomes partially decayed, but the process of decomposition is not completed. The bacteria necessary for decay need oxygen to grow, and the still, cold bog water is low in oxygen. Water and soil in a bog contain a lot of acid, which also slows the growth of bacteria. Because of these conditions, the remains of dead plants in the bog do not decompose in the normal way. Instead they turn into the substance known as **peat.**

Peat is a very useful material. Worked into the soil, it makes a good fertilizer. Made into blocks and dried, it can be burned for fuel. And left in the ground for thousands of years, it will eventually turn into another useful substance — coal.

The bryum mosses make up a very large group found in many parts of the world. This is the silvery bryum *(Bryum argentum)*, a moss that can grow in almost any kind of environment. Because it is not bothered by air pollution, it is a common moss in cities. The silvery bryum gets its name from the pale silvery color of the upper leaves on the gametophytes.

In addition to the sphagnums, there are hundreds of other mosses growing in almost all parts of the world. Here are a few more members of this large and varied group of plants.

Hairy caps are also very common mosses. They are large, with shoots up to 12 inches (30 centimeters) tall, and they grow in damp fields, meadows, and woodlands. Hairy caps get their English name from the hairs on their calyptras. The scientific name of the species shown here is *Polytrichum commune.*

Left: This is a rare moss with an unusual characteristic: it glows in the dark. The luminous moss *(Shistostega pennata)* grows in dimly lit places such as caves or crevices in rocks. Its protonema (shown in the inset picture) contains lens-like cells that reflect light. Because of the glowing light it gives off, this moss is sometimes called goblin's gold.

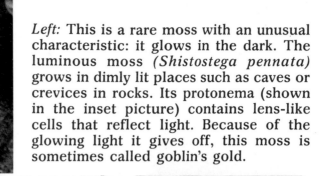

Above right: Another unusual and rarely seen moss is *Buxbaumia aphylla.* This small moss has very few leaves in the gametophyte stage. When its spores begin to ripen, the leaves disappear altogether. The strange shape of its spore capsules has earned this moss the nickname "bugs on a stick."

Right: A member of the group of cord mosses, *Funaria hygrometrica* has a long, cord-like seta that becomes twisted in dry weather and straightens out when the humidity is high. The moss's scientific name refers to this habit of responding to changes in humidity. *Hygrometrica* is a Latin word that means "water-measuring."

Hairy cap moss growing on the roof of a house. Like most mosses, this sturdy plant can make itself at home in many kinds of environments. Because mosses are so tough and so adaptable, they occupy a very special place in the world of plants.

GLOSSARY

alternation of generations—a system of reproduction in which a spore-producing generation of plants alternates with a generation that produces sex cells

antheridium (an-thuh-RID-ee-um)—the male reproductive organ of mosses and liverworts. The plural form of the word is **antheridia.**

archegonium (ar-keh-GO-nee-um)—the female reproductive organ of mosses and liverworts. The plural form of the word is **archegonia.**

bog—an area of wet, spongy land formed by sphagnum mosses growing in a shallow lake or pond

buds—small shoots on the protonema that develop into gametophytes

calyptra (kuh-LIP-truh)—the cap or lid on top of a spore capsule

chlorophyll (KLOR-uh-fihl)—the green coloring material in plants that makes photosynthesis possible

fertilization—the union of a male sperm cell and a female egg cell

foot—the structure that connects the seta of a sporophyte to the parent gametophyte

gametes (GAM-ehts)—male and female reproductive cells

gametophyte (geh-MEET-uh-fite)—a moss or liverwort in the gamete-producing stage of its reproductive cycle

gemmae (JEM-ee)—specialized pieces of tissue that can develop into new moss or liverwort gametophytes through the process of vegetative propagation. The singular form of the word is **gemma**.

operculum (o-PER-ku-luhm)—the structure under the calyptra that covers the opening of a spore capsule

peat (PEET)—material formed from partially decayed remains of sphagnum moss and other bog plants

peristome (PEAR-uh-stom)—the ring of tiny teeth around the opening of a spore capsule

photosynthesis (fot-uh-SIN-thuh-sis)—the process by which green plants make their own food

protonema (prot-uh-NEE-muh)—the thread-like structure that develops from a moss spore

rhizoids (RYE-zoids)—root-like threads that anchor a moss or liverwort to the substance on which it grows

seta (SEET-uh)—the stalk that connects a spore capsule to the parent gametophyte

spores—tiny one-celled reproductive bodies that develop into a new generation of gametophytes

vascular (VAS-ku-luhr) system—a network of channels that carry water through the tissues of a plant. Unlike most green plants, mosses and liverworts lack well-developed vascular systems.

vegetative propagation (VEJ-ih-tate-ive prop-uh-GAY-shun)—a method of reproduction that does not involve the union of sex cells. Many kinds of plants are capable of vegetative propagation as well as sexual reproduction.

46

About the Names Used in This Book

The mosses in this book are sometimes referred to by their scientific names as well as their common names. These Latin names are used by scientists all over the world. A moss may have many common names, but it can have only one scientific name. For example, the hairy cap moss shown in the book is sometimes called hair cap moss, bird wheat moss, or pigeon wheat moss. In Europe, Asia, and other parts of the world where it grows, the moss is known by another group of common names. But its scientific name, *Polytrichum commune,* is the same everywhere and can be recognized by people no matter what language they speak.

As you can see, scientific names are very useful not only to scientists but also to anyone who wants to learn about the natural world.

INDEX